My First
Pocket
Guide

D0283705

Vermont

By Carole Marsh

Correlates with Vermont's
FSLO
Framework of Standards
and Learning Opportunities

The GALLOPADE GANG

Carole Marsh	Kathy Zimmer	Cranston Davenport
Bob Longmeyer	Terry Briggs	Lisa Stanley
Chad Beard	Pat Newman	Antoinette Miller
Cecil Anderson	Billie Walburn	Victoria DeJoy
Steven Saint-Laurent	Jackie Clayton	Al Fortunatti
Jill Sanders	Pam Dufresne	Shery Kearney

Published by GALLOPADE INTERNATIONAL

www.thevermontexperience.com
800-536-2GET • www.gallopade.com

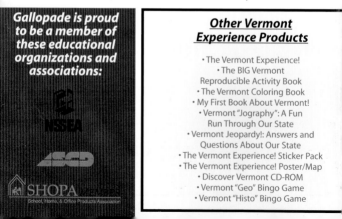

Gallopade is proud to be a member of these educational organizations and associations:

NSSEA

ASCD

SHOPA
School, Home, & Office Products Association

Other Vermont Experience Products

- The Vermont Experience!
- The BIG Vermont Reproducible Activity Book
- The Vermont Coloring Book
- My First Book About Vermont!
- Vermont "Jography": A Fun Run Through Our State
- Vermont Jeopardy!: Answers and Questions About Our State
- The Vermont Experience! Sticker Pack
- The Vermont Experience! Poster/Map
- Discover Vermont CD-ROM
- Vermont "Geo" Bingo Game
- Vermont "Histo" Bingo Game

A Word From the Author... (okay, a few words)...

Hi!
  Here's your own handy pocket guide about the great state of Vermont! It really will fit in a pocket—I tested it. And it really will be useful when you want to know a fact you forgot, to bone up for a test, or when your teacher says, "I wonder . . ." and you have the answer—instantly! Wow, I'm impressed!

Get smart, have fun!
  Carole Marsh

Vermont Basics

Vermont Geography

Vermont History

Vermont People

Vermont Places

Vermont Nature

Vermont Miscellany

Vermont Basics explores your state's symbols and their special meanings!

Vermont Geography digs up the what's where in your state!

Vermont History is like traveling through time to some of your state's great moments!

Vermont People introduces you to famous personalities and your next-door neighbors!

Vermont Places shows you where you might enjoy your next family vacation!

Vermont Nature - no preservatives here, just what Mother Nature gave to Vermont!

All the real fun stuff that we just HAD to save for its own section!

Who Named You?

Vermont's official state name is...

State Name

Vermont

Word Definition

OFFICIAL: appointed, authorized, or approved by a government or organization

Statehood: March 4, 1791

Vermont was the 14th state to join the Union.

Vermont's state-commemorative quarter was released in the year 2001. Look for it in cash registers everywhere!

Coccinella noemnotata is my name (that's Latin for ladybug)! What's YOURS?

4

What's In A Name?

The name "Vermont" originally comes from the French phrase *les monts verts,* or "the green mountains." French explorer Samuel de Champlain was the first European to see Vermont in 1609. He labeled the area "Vert Mont" on maps he drew, and the name was later shortened to "Vermont."

Champlain also discovered a lake that is named after him!

WHO Are You Calling Names?

Vermont is not the only name by which the state is recognized. Like many other states, Vermont has a nickname.

The Green Mountain State

Ethan Allen and his Green Mountain Boys helped to make this nickname famous during the Revolutionary War.

State Capital:
Montpelier

Established 1781

Capital of Vermont Since 1805

Until 1805, the Vermont state legislature had moved from town to town (14 different towns, to be exact!). Montpelier was chosen as the permanent capital on two conditions: the town had to donate land for the capitol, and the building had to be finished by September of 1808. The first State House was built at a cost of $9,000 but was torn down and replaced in 1838 at a cost of $132,000. The second State House was destroyed in 1857 by fire, and the third (and present) State House was built on the same site in 1859 at a cost of $150,000.

The 1857 fire was caused by the wood-burning heating system and burned everything inside the granite walls!

Word Definition

CAPITAL: a town or city that is the official seat of government
CAPITOL: the building in which the government officials meet

7

Who's in Charge Here?

Vermont's GOVERNMENT has three branches

LEGISLATIVE	EXECUTIVE	JUDICIAL

State Government

Also called the General Assembly Two Houses: The Senate (30 members) House of Representatives (150 members)	A governor, lieutenant governor, secretary of state, attorney general, state treasurer, and auditor of accounts	Supreme Court (a chief justice plus four associate justices) Probate Courts District Courts Superior Courts County Courts Court of Chancery

The number of legislators is determined by population, which is counted every ten years; the numbers above are certain to change as Vermont grows and prospers!

When you are 18 and register according to Vermont laws, you can vote! So please do! Your vote counts!

State Flag

State Flag

Vermont's current flag was adopted in 1923. It features a deep blue field, and a shield with a large pine tree, a cow, and sheaves of wheat. The cow and wheat both symbolize agriculture. The Green Mountains rise in the background behind the scene. The name "Vermont" and the motto "Freedom and Unity" are on a crimson banner below the shield. A stag's head is on top of the shield.

As you travel throughout Vermont, count the times you see the Vermont flag! Look for it on government vehicles, too!

State Seal

Vermont's state seal was designed by Reuben Dean in 1778 and adopted in 1779. It features a pine tree with 14 branches, which represent the original 13 states, plus Vermont. A row of wooded hills is also seen across the center of the seal. Wavy lines at the bottom and top represent water and sky, and a cow and sheaves of grain symbolize agriculture.

State Seal & Motto

Word Definition

MOTTO: a sentence, phrase, or word expressing the spirit or purpose of an organization or group

State Motto

Vermont's state motto is...

Freedom and Unity.

After the first seal wore out, another one was created in 1821.

Birds of a Feather

The hermit thrush is also known as the American nightingale, probably because of its beautiful, bell-like song. Hermit thrushes live on or near ground in pine woods, and feed on beetles, ants, caterpillars, some wild fruits, and weed seeds. They also lay greenish-blue, unmarked eggs. The hermit thrush became Vermont's state bird on June 1, 1941.

State Bird

Hermit Thrush
(Catharus guttatus)

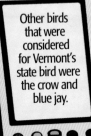

Other birds that were considered for Vermont's state bird were the crow and blue jay.

11

SUGAR MAPLE

"Woodman, spare that tree!"—George Pope Morris

(Acer saccharum)

Sugar maples are an important part of Vermont life. Every year, Vermonters produce maple syrup from the sugar maple trees, in a process called "sug'rin." The sap is collected from the trees, and then boiled in a sugarhouse to make the syrup. The sugar maple became Vermont's state tree on March 10, 1949.

RED CLOVER

Red clover was brought to the New World by the colonists, and now grows just about everywhere in Vermont. Red clover is fed to dairy cows to supply necessary nutrition, and honeybees turn the clover's nectar into sweet, light honey. The first part of its Latin name, *Trifolium*, means "three leaves." Red clover became Vermont's state flower on February 1, 1895.

State Flower

A lovelier flower on earth was never sown.
— William Wordsworth

(Trifolium pratense)

The other two contenders for the state flower title were the daisy and buttercup. Red clover won by a landslide!

RIDDLE:
If the state flower got mixed up with the state bird, what would you have?

ANSWER: A sweetly-singing flower with three leaves—it could happen!

Morgan Horse

(Equus caballus)

In 1788, a schoolteacher named Justin Morgan moved to Randolph, Vermont. In 1791, he brought a colt named Figure home from Massachusetts. Figure became famous as a hard worker who outperformed the other local horses. Figure was the first Morgan horse.

Morgans were popular for pulling carriages and for harness racing, until cars became popular. Then Morgan horses were turned into excellent saddle horses. On March 23, 1961, the Morgan horse became Vermont's state animal.

During the Civil War, the First Vermont Cavalry rode Morgan horses. Only 200 of the original 1,200 horses survived the war.

White Whale
(*Delphinapterus lucas* or *vermontanus*)

In 1849, railroad workers uncovered an unusual find. They discovered bones unlike any they had ever seen before. The bones were later identified as those of a beluga or white whale. The skeleton is about 12,500 years old, and was named Charlotte for the town near which it was found. In 1993, Vermont adopted Charlotte as its state fossil.

State Fossil

Vermont was once submerged under the Champlain Sea, a shallow part of the North Atlantic Ocean that disappeared about 10,000 years ago.

It's a whale of a symbol!

State Drink

Milk

MILK

Vermont adopted milk as its official beverage on April 22, 1983. At one time, cows actually outnumbered people in the state! Today, improved breeding and feeding techniques allow Vermonters to produce about 2.3 billion pounds (1 billion kilograms) of milk per year!

Dairy farming accounts for more than 80 percent of Vermont's annual farm income!

Granite, Marble, and Slate

State Rocks

In 1992, Vermont's legislature adopted three rocks that were important to the state's economy throughout its history: granite, marble, and slate. Granite is found all through eastern Vermont. In fact, the world's largest granite quarry is in Barre! Marble is plentiful in southwestern Vermont, and the Danby quarry is the world's largest underground quarry. Slate is also found in southwestern Vermont.

Granite is an igneous rock, and both marble and slate are metamorphic rocks.

Apple and Apple Pie

On May 10, 1999, Vermont designated the apple as the official state fruit, and apple pie as the official state pie. If you want to serve apple pie in Vermont, a "good faith" effort needs to be made to also serve one or more of the following:

State Fruit and Pie

a glass of milk

a slice of cheddar cheese weighing a minimum of 0.5 ounce (14 grams)

ICE CREAM

a large scoop of vanilla ice cream

Apples are good sources of fiber, Vitamins A and C, and potassium!

When do we eat?

State Insect

State
Insect

The honeybee became Vermont's state insect on July 1, 1978. Honeybees are important to Vermont farmers because they pollinate many of the crops grown in the state. Honeybees are social insects that live in large colonies, or hives. They also produce a yummy, sweet, healthful honey!

A typical honeybee hive has one queen, thousands of worker bees, and a few hundred drones. Drones are male bees, and workers are female bees. Only the queen bee lays eggs.

It's good to be the queen!

State Fishes

Cold Water Fish:
Brook Trout

(Salvelinus fontinalis)

The brook trout is the only trout that is native to Vermont streams. In 1978, when the Vermont state legislature chose the state fish, they actually chose two. The brook trout was the official cold water fish, and the walleye pike was the official warm water fish.

Warm Water Fish:
Walleye

The walleye is named for its unusual "marble" eyes, which are large and can look transparent in certain lights. The walleye was chosen as a state fish because it lives in Lake Champlain, Vermont's largest lake.

(Stizosedion vitreum vitreum)

RECIPE
Vermont Tasty Trout

Put a trout filet on foil. Drizzle with lemon juice. Sprinkle with salt and pepper. Add shredded smoked ham and broil fish until done.

Sounds fishy to me!

20

The State of
Vermont

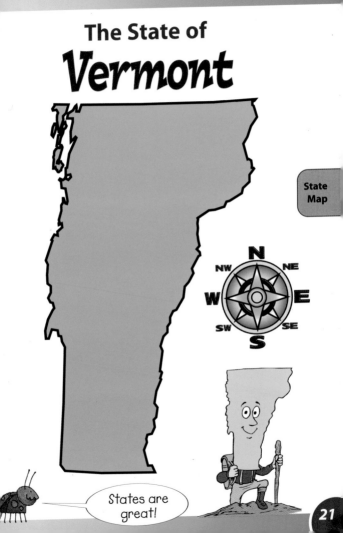

State
Map

States are great!

21

State Location

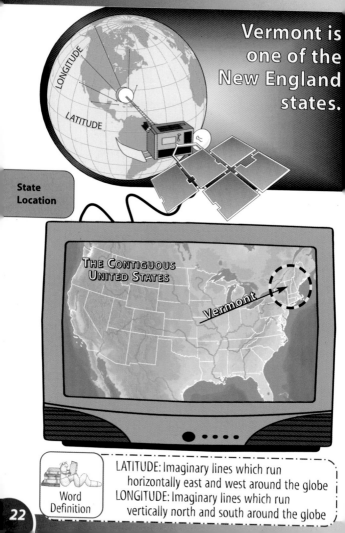

Vermont is one of the New England states.

LONGITUDE

LATITUDE

State Location

THE CONTIGUOUS UNITED STATES

Vermont

Word Definition

LATITUDE: Imaginary lines which run horizontally east and west around the globe
LONGITUDE: Imaginary lines which run vertically north and south around the globe

22

ON THE BORDER!

These border Vermont:

States: New Hampshire
Massachusetts
New York

Country: Canada

State Neighbors

Bodies of water: Lake Champlain
Connecticut River

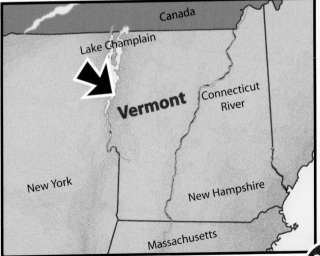

I'll Take the Low Road...

East-West, North-South, Area

Vermont stretches 156 miles (251 kilometers) from north to south—or south to north. Either way, it's a long walk!

Total Area: Approximately 9,615 square miles
(24,901 square kilometers)

Land Area: Approximately 9,249 square miles
(23,953 square kilometers)

Vermont is 37 miles (60 kilometers) from east to west—or west to east. Either way, it's *still* a long walk!

This is a compass rose. It helps you find the right direction on a map!

24

You Take the High Road!

HIGHEST POINT
Mount Mansfield—4,393 feet (1,339 meters)
above sea level

Mount Mansfield was named after the Mansfield township, which was named for Lord Mansfield of England. Lord Mansfield was the chief justice and the earl of Mansfield in the mid-1700s.

LOWEST POINT
Lake Champlain in Franklin County—95 feet
(30 meters) above sea level.

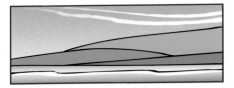

I'm County-ing on Vermont's Towns!

State Towns

Vermont is divided into 14 counties, although the counties are mainly law enforcement and judicial jurisdictions. Vermont is divided into more than 230 towns, each with its own local government. Most local governmental business is conducted at town meetings.

Word Definition

COUNTY:
an administrative subdivision of a state or territory

1, 2, 3, 4, 5...

6, 7, 8, 9, 10...

Natural Resources

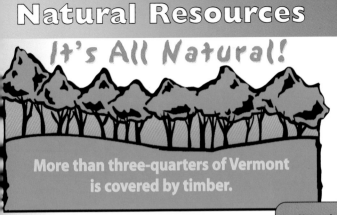

It's All Natural!

More than three-quarters of Vermont is covered by timber.

Word Definition

NATURAL RESOURCES: things that exist in or are formed by nature

Minerals and rocks:

Iron Pyrite
Kaolinite
Gold
Silver
Pegmatite
Mica
Granite
Marble

Pegmatite is usually found alongside granite deposits!

Rock and Roll!

27

Weather, Or Not?!

Vermont winters are usually long and cold, and summers are typically short but warm. Vermont's temperatures can drop to -34°F (-37°C) in the winter and top 90°F (32°C) in the summer, although there are few really hot summer days.

Weather

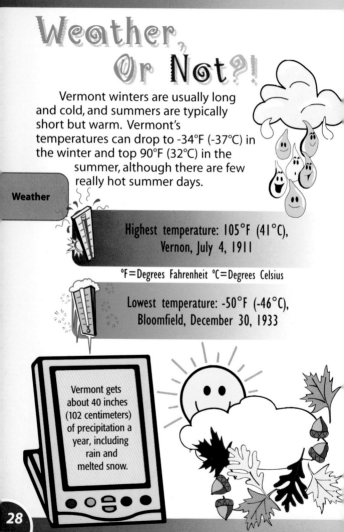

Highest temperature: 105°F (41°C), Vernon, July 4, 1911

°F=Degrees Fahrenheit °C=Degrees Celsius

Lowest temperature: -50°F (-46°C), Bloomfield, December 30, 1933

Vermont gets about 40 inches (102 centimeters) of precipitation a year, including rain and melted snow.

Topography

BACK ON TOP

Vermonters call outsiders "flatlanders" for good reason! The mean elevation of the state is 1,000 feet (305 meters) above sea level! Vermont is full of mountains, plateaus, hills, and uplands. Much of the state is covered by the Green Mountains for which it's named!

Word Definition

TOPOGRAPHY: the detailed mapping of the features of a small area or district

The Taconic section of Vermont contains the state's largest marble deposits!

Sea Level

100 m 328 ft

200 m 656 ft

500 m 1,640 ft

1,000 m 3,281 ft

2,000 m 6,562 ft

5,000 m 16,404 ft

29

King of the Hill

Mountains

- Mount Mansfield
- Killington Mountain
- Mount Ellen
- Camels Hump
- Monadnock Mountain
- Mount Ascutney
- Mount Equinox
- The Dome

Mountain Ranges

- Northfield Mountains
- Worcester Mountains
- Green Mountains
- White Mountains
- Lowell Mountains
- Taconic Range

Climb every mountain...

A River Runs Through It!

Here are some of Vermont's major rivers:

- **Connecticut River**
- **Otter Creek**
- **Mettawee River**
- **Winooski River**
- **Ottauquechee River**
- **Lamoille River**
- **Missisquoi River**
- **Passumpsic River**
- **White River**
- **West River**

Rivers

Otter Creek (100 miles, or 161 kilometers, long) is the longest river in Vermont!

Grab a paddle!

Gone Fishin'

Major Lakes

Major lakes in Vermont include:

- **LAKE CHAMPLAIN**
- **LAKE MEMPHREMAGOG**
- **LAKE BOMOSEEN**
- **LAKE OF THE CLOUDS**
- **CHITTENDEN RESERVOIR**
- **SOMERSET RESERVOIR**

Lake of the Clouds is the highest lake in Vermont. It's about 4,000 feet (1,219 meters) up the slopes of Mount Mansfield!

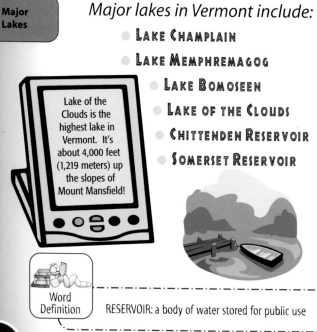

Word Definition

RESERVOIR: a body of water stored for public use

ARE YOU A CITY MOUSE... OR A COUNTRY MOUSE?

Have you heard of these wonderful Vermont town, city, or crossroad names? Perhaps you can start your own list!

MAJOR CITIES:
- Burlington
- Rutland
- Barre
- Montpelier

UNIQUE NAMES:
- Derby
- Georgia
- Jamaica
- Jericho
- Moscow
- Paper Mill Village
- Peru
- Proctor

Transportation

Major Interstate Highways

There are about 14,251 miles (22,934 kilometers) of roads and highways in Vermont, of which about 320 miles (515 kilometers) are part of the interstate highway system.
I-89, I-91, I-93

Railroads

Vermont's first railroad was completed in 1849, and was mostly used as a link to Boston, Massachusetts. Today, there are about 544 miles (875 kilometers) of railroad track in Vermont.

Major Airports

Vermont has three major commercial airports, at Burlington, Rutland, and Barre-Montpelier.

Water Routes

There are several ferry routes across Lake Champlain between Vermont and its neighbor New York.

Timeline

1609	Samuel de Champlain claims the Vermont area for France
1724	English colonists from Massachusetts build the first permanent settlement at Fort Dummer
1741	King of England gives Vermont to New Hampshire
1775	Ethan Allen and the Green Mountain Boys capture Fort Ticonderoga
1777	Vermont declares itself an independent state with the name of New Connecticut
1791	Vermont becomes the 14th U.S. state
1805	Montpelier becomes the state capital
1823	Champlain-Hudson Canal links Vermont to New York City
1850	Vermont legislature nullifies the Fugitive Slave Law
1864	Confederate forces attack St. Albans
1881	Chester A. Arthur becomes the 21st president
1909	First Boy Scout Club is organized in Barre by William F. Milne, a Scottish immigrant
1923	Calvin Coolidge becomes the 30th president
1947	Vermont's state police force is organized
1985	Madeleine Kunin is elected the first woman governor of Vermont
1991	Vermont celebrates its bicentennial
2001	Vermont enters the 21st century!

Early History

Here come the humans!

Early History

Until recently, scientists have believed that the first humans came to North America about 14,000 years ago. These people crossed over a land bridge between Siberia and Alaska, and then spread out across the North American continent. New evidence now suggests that people may have first arrived at the Americas 15,000, 20,000 or even 30,000 years ago! New evidence also indicates that instead of one single migration across the land bridge in Alaska, people may have come to this continent in several waves, and some of them also came across the Atlantic Ocean from Europe!

These early people were nomadic hunters who traveled in small bands. They camped when seasons offered hunting, fishing, and fruit and nut gathering.

36

Early Indians

Native Americans Once Ruled!

Remains of temporary Native American settlements can be found at Orwell, Newbury, Swanton, and Vernon. Along the Connecticut River at Bellows Falls are ancient Indian petroglyphs. Until the 1500s, the Vermont area was controlled by Algonquian-speaking tribes; Iroquois tribes began to move into Vermont from nearby New York in the years before the arrival of European explorers. The Native American population was never very large in Vermont. They supported themselves mainly by hunting and fishing.

Early Indians

Word Definition

WAMPUM: beads, pierced and strung, used by Indians as money or for ornaments

Exploration

Land Ho!

The French were the first Europeans to see Vermont. Samuel de Champlain arrived in 1609, sent to explore the New World by the king of France. Champlain claimed the Vermont area for France. The French were interested in establishing fur trade with the

Algonquian-speaking tribes in the area and built a few military posts. However, the French did not establish any permanent settlements. Vermont remained a wilderness for many years.

Champlain wrote about a lake filled with beautiful islands. Which lake do you think he was writing about?

Settlement at Last!

Home, Sweet Home

For more than 100 years after Champlain's first visit, almost no Europeans settled in Vermont. The French built Fort Saint Anne in 1666 on Isle La Motte in Lake Champlain but soon abandoned it.

Dutch settlers from Albany, New York, set up a temporary outpost at Chimney Point in 1690. The French built forts at Crown Point and Ticonderoga (which they called Fort Carillon) in the mid-1700s.

Settlement at Last!

In 1724, the English established Fort Dummer in northeastern Vermont in order to protect Massachusetts settlers from raids by the French and local Native Americans. Fort Dummer was the first permanent European settlement in the Vermont area and was located where Brattleboro is today.

Although not many European settlers lived in Vermont, the wilderness was often a battleground where the French and English fought for control of North America!

DAIRY PRODUCTS

At one time, cows actually outnumbered people in Vermont! Dairying has been an important part of the Vermont economy for a long time. Until the mid-19th century, sheep were a main source of income for Vermont farmers. However, it became cheaper to raise sheep in the Western range lands, and the Vermont farming system switched from raising sheep to raising dairy cows. Cattle were natural grazers, and it was easy to convert many of the earlier sheep farms into dairy farms.

Key Product

The developing railroad systems and growing population centers south of Vermont made milk and other dairy products a profitable business for Vermonters. By 1900, there were more than 200,000 cows on Vermont farms. Today, Vermont leads New England in dairy production!

MILK

The Mighty Mysterious Monster of Lake Champlain!

Believe it or not: A mysterious monster lives in Lake Champlain! The Abenaki Indians told tales of Tatoskok, a large monster living in Lake Champlain. In 1609, Samuel de Champlain himself reported seeing "a 20-foot serpent as thick as a barrel with a head like a horse." (Although Champlain apparently saw this beast elsewhere, people have believed for years he saw it in Lake Champlain.)

Champ (as the beast it now called) has been sighted hundreds of times in Lake Champlain. People have even taken photographs of what they believe is the mysterious lake monster!

Some believe that Champ is a water-dwelling dinosaur. Others think it's a zeuglodon, an ancient snake-like whale that's supposed to be extinct! Whatever Champ is, he's a mystery (and there are probably more than one of him)!

Freedom! Freedom!

Some settlers in the New World felt that England ignored their ideas and concerns. In 1775, the colonies went to war with England. On July 4, 1776, the Declaration of Independence was signed.

Revolution

Ethan Allen and his Green Mountain Boys were very important in the struggle for independence. In 1775, the Green Mountain Boys captured Fort Ticonderoga without firing a single shot! The Boys captured another British outpost at Crown Point, and a British ship on the Canadian Richelieu River.

The only Revolutionary War battle on Vermont soil was in Hubbardton, in July of 1777. Both the Green Mountain Boys and the British suffered losses. The next month, the Boys and some troops from Massachusetts won the Battle of Bennington.

The victory at the Battle of Bennington led to a later victory at the Battle of Saratoga. The Battle of Saratoga was the turning point of the war!

Slaves and Slavery

The 1800s were a time of many reform movements in Vermont. Vermonters were especially passionate about the abolition of slavery. In 1777, Vermont drafted the first constitution that outlawed slavery, and slavery has remained illegal since then. Many Vermont households were stops along the Underground Railroad, the secret route that took many slaves from the South to freedom in Canada.

In 1837, the Vermont legislature sent resolutions to the U.S. Senate protesting the annexation of Texas as a slave state. In fact, by 1837 there were 89 local anti-slavery societies in Vermont, with more than 5,000 members! In 1860, nearly three-quarters of Vermont's votes went to Abraham Lincoln, even though his opponent was native Vermonter Stephen Douglas!

In 1865, the 13th Amendment abolished slavery in the United States.

Slaves and Slavery

Word Definition

ABOLITIONIST: person who believed slavery was wrong and should be ended

Brother

The Civil War was fought between the American states. The argument was over states' rights to make their own decisions, including whether or not to own slaves. Some of the southern states began to secede (leave) the Union.

They formed the Confederate States of America. Vermont was the first state to offer troops in the Civil War.

> **The Civil War**

Vermonters contributed more than $9 million to the Union war effort, more than 30,000 Vermont men and 1,200 Morgan horses for the Union cavalry. In August of 1864, a group of Confederate soldiers sneaked into St. Albans and robbed three local banks. The soldiers dashed for the Canadian border with more than $200,000. The St. Albans bank robberies were the northernmost activity in the Civil War!

Word Definition

RECONSTRUCTION: the recovery and rebuilding period following the Civil War

vs. Brother

The Civil War was also called the War Between the States. Soldiers often found themselves fighting against former friends and neighbors, even brother against brother. Those who did survive often went home without an arm, leg, or both, since amputation was the "cure" for most battlefield wounds. More Americans were killed during the Civil War than during World Wars I and II together!

The Civil War

In 1863, the Emancipation Proclamation, given by U.S. President Abraham Lincoln, freed the slaves still under Confederate control. Some slaves became sharecroppers; others went to Northern states to work in factories.

Get It In Writing!

1776
Declaration of Independence

1777
Vermont's first constitution

1786
Vermont's second constitution

1789
U.S. Constitution

1790
The U.S.'s first patent, issued to
Samuel Hopkins for making potash out
of wood ashes

1793
Vermont's third and present constitution

1940
Social Security Check #000-000-001
for $22.54 issued to Ida M. Fuller

Immigrants

WELCOME TO AMERICA!

People have come to Vermont from other states and many other countries on almost every continent! As time goes by, Vermont's population grows more diverse. This means that people of different races and from different cultures and ethnic backgrounds have moved to Vermont.

In the past, many immigrants have come to Vermont from Canada and European countries including Ireland, Scotland, Spain, Sweden, and Wales. More recently, people have migrated to Vermont from Mexico, Asia, Africa, and the former Soviet Union. Only a certain number of immigrants are allowed to move to America each year. Many of these immigrants eventually become U.S. citizens.

Immigrants

1816

A year of famine occurs, with snow
or frost every month

1857

The second state capitol is destroyed by fire

1864

Confederate soldiers raid St. Albans

**Disasters &
Catastrophes!**

1927

Severe flooding of the Winooski River and
branches of the Connecticut River kill several
and cause millions of dollars' worth of damage

1938

A hurricane kills five and causes
more than $10 million in damage

1973

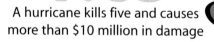

The worst flood since 1927 causes an estimated
$65 million in damage

1777

Vermont's constitution
outlaws slavery

1850

Vermont state legislature nullifies
the Fugitive Slave Law

1852

Manufacture and sale of
intoxicating liquor is outlawed

Legal Stuff

1896

Vermont enacts the first absentee
voting law in the U.S.

1970

Environmental Control Law, Act 250,
passed by Vermont state legislature

1976

Governor Thomas Salmon grants official
status to Abenaki Indians, qualifying
them for certain federal benefits

1804

The first educational society is established in Pawlet

1814

Emma Willard establishes first school of higher education for women in Middlebury

Women & Children

1823

First normal school exclusively for teacher preparation founded in Concord

1909

First Boy Scout Club founded in Barre

1954

Consuelo N. Bailey becomes first woman in the U.S. elected lieutenant governor

Wars

Fight! Fight! Fight!
Wars that impacted Vermont:

- French and Indian War
- Revolutionary War
- War of 1812
- Mexican-American War
- Civil War
- Spanish-American War
- World War I
- World War II
- Korean War
- Vietnam War
- Persian Gulf War

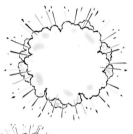

Wars

While visitors come to Vermont year-round, the most popular time to visit the Green Mountain State is during the last two weeks of September and the first two weeks of October. This is called the foliage season, because it is when the lush forests of Vermont change to brilliant fall colors. It gets so crowded in the state that inns and hotels have increased "foliage rates," and rooms are usually fully booked six months in advance! Vermont highways are jammed with "leaf peepers," as the Vermonters call the foliage enthusiasts.

Frequently Famous Fall Foliage

Indian Tribes

Algonquian-speaking
Abenaki
Mahican
Pennacook

Iroquois from New York

Many of the place names in Vermont can be traced to different Native American words. For example, "Winooski" comes from the Abenaki word for "wild onion place," and "Jamaica" comes from the Natick word for "beaver."

Indian
Tribes

The Native Americans of Vermont could not have known that the coming of the Europeans would mean an end to the way of life they had known for hundreds of years.

Here, There, Everywhere!

Samuel de Champlain was a French explorer and cartographer. He came to the Vermont area in 1609, on an expedition to find furs and establish fur trade. Champlain made friends with the Algonquian-speaking Indians and joined them in a raid on the Iroquois in New York. While he was on this raid, he became the first European to reach Lake Champlain (which he named for himself), and he claimed the Vermont area for France.

Explorers and Settlers

Jacobus de Warm led British soldiers into Vermont from Albany, New York, in 1690. De Warm founded a fort at Chimney Point, west of present-day Middlebury.

Bon Voyage!

State Founders

Founding Fathers

Benning Wentworth—first Royal Governor of New Hampshire; starting with Bennington in 1749, Wentworth sold large tracts of land in Vermont to speculators; these New Hampshire Grants brought many settlers to Vermont

Thomas Chittenden—helped to write Vermont's constitution; first governor of the independent state of Vermont; first state governor of Vermont

Joseph Smith—born in Vermont; in 1830 published the *Book of Mormon* and founded the Church of Jesus Christ of Latter-day Saints

Ben Cohen and Jerry Greenfield—founded Ben and Jerry's Ice Cream in 1978

Founding Mothers

State Founders

Ann Story—after the death of her husband Amos, moved with her children to the "New Hampshire Grants" (Vermont) around 1775; her home was used as a message drop and shelter for patriots during the American Revolution; became known as the "Mother of the Green Mountain Boys"

Blanche Honneggar-Moyse—co-founder of the Marlboro School of Music; founded the New England Bach Festival

Lemuel Haynes—in 1783, became the first African-American to be a pastor of a white congregation; had also fought with the Minutemen in 1775; was with Ethan Allen when he captured Fort Ticonderoga

Martin Freeman—in 1854, was appointed Professor at the Allegheny Institute near Pittsburgh, Pennsylvania; was appointed President of the school in 1856, becoming the first African-American to be president of a college

Famous African-Americans

Austin Hazard, Charles Wentworth, Howard Greeley, Israel Hunter, Isaac Williams, Peter Brace, Robert Brown, Reuben Burton, Thomas H. Green, Sylvester Mero, and Jackson Sheldon—Vermonter members of Company B, 54th Massachusetts Infantry Volunteers; this military unit fought in the Spanish and American War and the Civil War; a monument in Coventry honors the unit

Ghosts

DID SOMEONE SAY BOO!?

Converse Hall at the *University of Vermont* is said to be haunted by the ghost of a medical student who committed suicide in the 1920s.

Room 2 at *Waterbury's Old Stage Coach Inn* is reportedly haunted by the ghost of Margaret Spencer.

Ghosts

Emily's Bridge in *Stowe* is named after the ghost that haunts it. A flickering white light is often seen there, and many believe it is the ghost of a woman who hanged herself there after her fiancé left her.

DO YOU BELIEVE IN GHOSTS?

57

Andrea Mead—won the first Olympic gold medals awarded to an American woman in 1952

Tad Coffin—won the first American gold medal in the Olympic three-day individual equestrian (horse) event in 1976

Bill Koch—won the first American medal in an Olympic nordic skiing event

Rudyard Kipling—while living in Vermont in the 1890s, invented the sport of snow golf

 Sports Stuff

Barbara Cochran—won a gold medal for the slalom run alpine skiing event in the 1972 Olympics

 **John LeClair**—hockey player; played for the Montreal Canadiens and the Philadelphia Flyers; the first native Vermonter to play for the NHL

Patty Sheehan—professional golfer; the 13th inductee to the LPGA Hall of Fame

Inventors

Samuel Morey—invented the first internal-combustion engine with a carburetor

Thaddeus Fairbanks—invented and patented the first platform scale; invented a hot water heater and a draft mechanism for furnaces

John Deere—inventor and manufacturer; invented the first steel plow; manufactured plows and tractors at Deere and Company

Thomas Davenport—invented the first electric motor on record; also invented an electric train, printing press, and piano

James Sargent—invented the "nonpickable" combination lock and the time lock; invented railway semaphore signals and automatic fire alarms

Inventors

James Hartness—helped to standardize screw threads

Elisha Graves Otis—invented safety devices for elevators; patented a steam elevator; founded the Otis elevator company

Horace Wells—was the first to use laughing gas as an anaesthetic when extracting a tooth

Isaac Fisher—invented sandpaper

Authors

- **Sara Cleghorn**—reformer and writer; wrote poetry, fiction, and articles about social concerns

- **John Dewey**—philosopher, educator, and author; wrote *The School and Society, Experience and Nature, Experience and Education,* and *Freedom and Culture;* was an advisor to various countries' educational systems

- **Robert Frost**—poet; founder of the Bread Loaf School in Middlebury (1920); won four Pulitzer Prizes in poetry; was the Poet Laureate of Vermont (1961)

- **Dorothy Canfield Fisher**—author of fiction and nonfiction books including *The Squirrel Cage* and *American Portraits*

- **Abby Maria Hemenway**—wrote the five-volume history of Vermont titled *Vermont Historical Gazetteer*

Authors

- **Sinclair Lewis**—novelist; author of *Babbitt, Elmer Gantry,* and others; was the first American to win the Nobel Prize in literature (1930)

- **Aleksandr Isayevich Solzhenitsyn**—exiled from the U.S.S.R. in 1974 and moved to Vermont; author and historian

Royall Tyler was the first American to write a comedic play. He wrote *The Contrast* in 1787.

- **Maria von Trapp**—her award-winning *Story of the Trapp Family Singers* was made into the stage musical and movie *The Sound of Music*

- **Rudyard Kipling**—author of *Jungle Book* and others; lived in Dummerston from 1892 to 1896

Artists

Norman Rockwell—painter and illustrator; famous for his *Saturday Evening Post* cover illustrations; illustrated several other major publications; many of his models were Vermonters

William Morris Hunt—painter; his work hangs in the Metropolitan Museum of Art

Larkin Goldsmith Mead—sculptor; designed the Lincoln Tomb in Springfield, Illinois; created statues of Ethan Allen for the Vermont Capitol and for the Capitol in Washington, D.C.

William Rutherford Mead—architect; designed the Rhode Island State House and the Boston Public Library; president of the American Academy in Rome (1909–1927)

Hiram Powers—sculptor; created statues of Benjamin Franklin and Thomas Jefferson for the Capitol in Washington, D.C.

Thomas Waterman Wood—painter who depicted African-Americans in the Civil War; established the Wood Gallery of Art in Montpelier

Artists

Question? Which Vermont artist also illustrated a printing of Mark Twain's *Tom Sawyer*?

Answer: Norman Rockwell

Very Important People

Myra Colby Bradwell—lawyer and editor; became the first American woman attorney when she was admitted to the Illinois bar in 1892

John Stark—fought in the French and Indian War; Revolutionary War patriot; served with the Vermont militia at the Battle of Bennington; coined the phrase "Live free or die"

Zerah Colburn—teacher and clergyman; mathematical genius

Paul P. Harris—founded the National Association of Rotary Clubs in 1910, while living in Vermont

John Morgan—his horse Figure was the first of the Morgan horses

Very Important People

George Perkins Marsh—author, linguist, and diplomat; opened a law practice in Burlington; U.S. representative (1843–1849); ambassador to Turkey (1849–1854)

Clarina Howard Nichols—her editorials influenced the women's suffrage movement; lobbied for laws granting more rights to women

Carrie Kilgore—teacher, lawyer, advocate of women's rights; first woman to graduate from the University of Pennsylvania Law School (1883)

Ira Allen—brother of Ethan Allen; wrote the preamble to the constitution of the independent state of Vermont; donated land to build the University of Vermont

William Alwyn "Snowflake" Bentley—first to photograph snowflakes through a microscope; proved that each snowflake has a unique shape

Samuel Herrick—Revolutionary War officer; captured Skeensborough, New York; fought at the Battle of Bennington; gained control of Lake George; drove the British from Mounts Hope, Independence and Defiance; forced the British to evacuate Ticonderoga

William Griffith Wilson—co-founder of Alcoholics Anonymous

George Dewey—U.S. naval officer; served under Admiral Farragut in the Civil War; commanded the Asian squadron during the Spanish-American War

More Very
Important
People

Ralph Edward Flanders—supported the Truman Doctrine and the Marshall Plan; led the move to censure Senator Joseph McCarthy during the anticommunist hearings

Matthew Lyon—an officer in the Green Mountain Boys; U.S. representative (1797–1801)

Alden Partridge—founded the first private military college at Norwich in 1819

The college founded by Captain Partridge offered the first Civil Engineering course in the U.S.

Political Leaders

Sherman Adams—U.S. representative (1945–1949); governor (1949–1953); assistant to President Dwight D. Eisenhower (1953–1958)

Chester A. Arthur—21st president (1881–1885)

Warren Robinson Austin—U.S. senator (1931–1946); head of the first U.S. delegation to the United Nations (1946–1953).

Jacob Collamer—state supreme court judge (1833–1842); U.S. representative (1843–1849); U.S. postmaster general (1849–1850); U.S. senator (1855–1865)

Political Leaders

Calvin Coolidge—30th president (1923–1929); lieutenant governor; his December 6, 1923 State of The Union Address was the first presidential address broadcast on radio

Stephen A. Douglas—lawyer and politician who practiced law in Illinois; as a presidential candidate, engaged in famous debates with fellow candidate Abraham Lincoln

George Franklin Edmunds—served in both the Vermont legislature and Congress; helped draft the Civil Rights Act (1875) and the Sherman Antitrust Act (1890)

Good Guys, Patriots, and Heros

Ethan Allen—founder and leader of the Green Mountain Boys; American revolutionary and patriot; created the Green Mountain Boys to fight off New Yorkers attempting to drive Vermonters off their land; captured Fort Ticonderoga in 1775; captured by the British in a raid on Montreal; held prisoner for more than two years; fought for Vermont statehood after the end of the Revolution

Seth Warner—helped to found the Green Mountain Boys; led the forces that captured Crown Point (1775); helped John Stark plan the Battle of Bennington; captured ships in which British General Burgoyne would have escaped at Lake George; led the Green Mountain Boys after the capture of Ethan Allen by the British

Good Guys, Patriots, and Heros

Justin Smith Morrill—helped to create the predecessors to state colleges; as a U.S. representative, he sponsored the Land Grant Colleges Act of 1862, which provided public lands for agricultural colleges; also helped to create the Library of Congress and the Washington Monument

Justin Morrill served 44 consecutive years in Congress!

Churches and Schools

Keeping the Faith

Old First Church, Bennington—built in 1805; burial site of Robert Frost

Center Shaftsbury Baptist Church, Shaftsbury—built in 1846; home of the Shaftsbury Historical Society Museum

United Church of Dorset and East Rupert, Dorset—19th-century church built of local marble

United Baptist Church, East Poultney—built in 1805

Old South Congregational Church, Windsor—built in 1798

Old Round Church, Richmond—a 16-sided church topped by an octagonal (8-sided) belfry; built in 1813

SCHOOLS

Middlebury College, Middlebury—founded in 1800

University of Vermont, Burlington—chartered in 1791; Vermont's first school of higher education

Johnson State College, Johnson—founded in 1818

Green Mountain College, Poultney—founded in 1834

Bennington College, Bennington—founded in 1932

School for International Training, Brattleboro—founded in 1964

Churches and Schools

Historic Sites and Parks

Emma Willard House National Historic Landmark,
Middlebury—site of the Middlebury Female Seminary
established in 1814 by Emma Willard

Chester A. Arthur Historic Site, Fairfield—a 35-acre
(14.2-hectare) park devoted to the 21st president; a
replica of Arthur's simple clapboard
childhood home; the brick church
his father preached in is also
located in the park

Coolidge Birthplace and
Coolidge Homestead,
Plymouth Notch—birthplace
and childhood home of the
30th president; Coolidge's
father administered the presidential oath at the
Homestead in 1923, a few hours after the death of
President Harding

Old Constitution House, Windsor—the
18th-century tavern where representatives met
in 1777 to adopt Vermont's first constitution;
has been moved from its original location twice

**Historic
Sites and
Parks**

Chimney Point Historic Site, near Middlebury—
exhibits about the original native peoples and early
French settlers

Green Mountain National Forest—southern and
central Vermont; established in 1911

Historical Homes

Park-McCullough House, Bennington—completed in 1865; was home to two Vermont governors, Hiland Hall and John G. McCullough

Homer Noble Farm, South Shaftsbury—built in 1769; Robert Frost bought it in 1920

Hildene, Manchester— home of Robert Todd Lincoln, Abraham Lincoln's only child to survive to adulthood

Wilson Castle, Proctor—a mid-1800s castle in the center of a 150-acre (60.7-hectare) estate; open for visitors

John Strong Mansion, Middlebury—built in the 1790s; has four "hidey holes," each big enough to hold several people; the hiding places were built for refuge from Indian attacks, and from bears (a group of bears had come into Strong's first house looking for food!)

Home, Sweet Home!

Rowland Thomas Robinson House, Ferrisburg—now the Rokeby Museum; home of the founder of the Vermont Anti-Slavery Society; his home was a stop on the Underground Railroad

Hyde Log Cabin, Grand Isle—built in 1783; considered the nation's oldest log cabin still standing in its original condition

A few of Vermont's famous Forts

● **Fort Dummer,** south of Brattleboro—built in 1724; was flooded by a dam built across the river 200 years later

● **Fort Saint Anne,** Isle La Motte—built by the French in 1666 to protect French colonists from the marauding Iroquois

● **Mount Independence,** Orwell—fortified by the Americans after they had captured Fort Ticonderoga; contains ruins of fortifications and gun batteries

Battlefield

Forts and a
Battlefield

● **Hubbardton Battlefield,** Hubbardton—the site of the only Revolutionary War battle to take place on Vermont soil; on July 7, 1777, the Green Mountain Boys met up with British and Hessian troops; both sides suffered heavy losses, but the Americans stopped the British pursuit of the main American force evacuating Fort Ticonderoga

Libraries

Check out the following special Vermont libraries! (Do you have a library card? Have you worn it out yet?!)

Brookfield Library—founded in 1791; is the oldest continually operating library in Vermont

Brooks Memorial Library, Brattleboro—largest library in the state

Vermont Historical Society Library, Montpelier

Bailey/Howe Library, Burlington—located on the University of Vermont campus; the largest university library in the state

Memorial Library, Dorset—housed in a 1790 tavern

Rutland Free Library, Rutland—designed by Ammi B. Young to house the post office and federal court

State Library, Montpelier

Libraries

There are 197 tax-supported libraries in Vermont, which circulate more than 6 books per resident each year!

Zoos and Attractions

Fairbanks Museum and Planetarium, St. Johnsbury—founded in 1889

Discovery Museum, Essex Junction—features hands-on and interactive exhibits

Green Mountain Audubon Nature Center and Birds of Vermont Museum, south of Richmond

Ben and Jerry's Ice Cream Factory, Waterbury—tours include a slide show telling the story of Ben and Jerry's enterprise

Morse Farm Sugar Shack, near Montpelier—see the sugaring-off process

Vermont Institute of Natural Science, Woodstock—dedicated to environmental education; the Vermont Raptor Center contains more than 20 species of owls, hawks, and eagles

Vermont State Craft Center, Middlebury—see the work of more than 250 Vermont craftspeople

Zoos and Attractions

LION

Bennington Museum, Bennington—specializes in the region's art and history; also exhibits the flag flown at the Battle of Bennington, believed to be the oldest surviving Stars and Stripes

Vermont Marble Exhibit, Proctor—displays locally quarried marble and shows the process by which the raw material is turned into carved and polished finished products

New England Maple Museum, Pittsford—exhibits on the history of Vermont sugaring, from the time before European settlement

Franklin County Museum, St. Albans—occupies an 1861 nine-room schoolhouse; contains local artifacts including those from the Confederate raid in 1864

Vermont Museum, Montpelier—permanent and rotating exhibits illustrate Vermont's way of life from prehistory to the present day

Museums

SCHOOL

Lest We Forget

Bennington Battle Monument, Bennington—a 306-foot (93.3-meter) tall dolomite obelisk commemorating the 1777 battle that occurred 2 miles (3.22 kilometers) away in New York

Hubbardton Battlefield Monument, Hubbardton—a spire of solid Vermont marble

Greenmount Cemetery, Burlington—said to be the burial place of Ethan Allen; a 42-foot (12.8-meter) tall statue of Allen stands over the burial site

St. Anne's Shrine, Isle La Motte—a granite statue of Champlain stands where he is believed to have landed in 1609

Monuments and Memorials

Soldier and Sailors Memorial, Barre—located in City Park; carved from local granite

Joseph Smith Monument, South Royalton—marks the birthplace of the founder of the Mormon faith

The Arts

Chaffee Art Center, Rutland—formerly the 1892 home of marble magnate George Chaffee

Shelburne Museum, Shelburne—a complex of 37 buildings, chock full of folk art

St. Johnsbury Athenaeum, St. Johnsbury—art gallery built in 1873; contains a large collection of Hudson River School paintings

Brattleboro Museum and Art Center, Brattleboro—includes pipe organs made by Jacob Esty

The Arts

Robert Hull Fleming Museum of Art, Burlington—located at the University of Vermont Bennington Museum

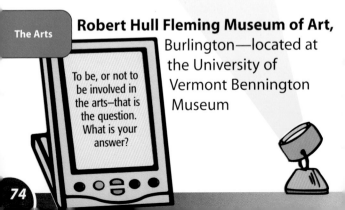

To be, or not to be involved in the arts–that is the question. What is your answer?

Covered Bridges

Vermont has about 100 covered bridges—that's more than any other state!

Montgomery—known as the "Covered Bridge Capital of Vermont"; has seven covered bridges, including the Longley, Comstock, and Fuller; most are still used daily

Shoreham Covered Railroad Bridge, Larrabee's Point—108-meter (32.9-meter) long covered bridge built by the Rutland Railroad in 1897

Fisher Covered Railroad Bridge, Stowe—built in 1908; the last covered railroad bridge still in regular use in Vermont

Windsor-Cornish Covered Bridge, Windsor—460 feet (140 meters) long; the longest covered bridge in the United States; connects New Hampshire and Vermont across the Connecticut River

Baltimore Covered Bridge, Springfield—built in 1870; connected Springfield to nearby Baltimore (Vermont)

Scott Covered Bridge, Bellows Falls—crosses the West River; built in 1870

Columbia Covered Bridge, Lemington—crosses over into New Hampshire

> Covered Bridges

Scenic Roads

Take the Long Way Home!

Vermont 100, from Wilmington to Newport—the "Main Street" of the Green Mountains; passes through many Vermont villages

Smugglers Notch, between Stowe and Jeffersonville—passes the Trapp Family Lodge on the way to Mount Mansfield; goes through Smugglers Notch State Park

Victory Basin Drive, through the Victory Basin wetlands—surrounded by the 13,000-acre (5,261-hectare) Victory State Forest

Champlain Islands, between Colchester and Alburg—follows the main route through the chain of islands in Lake Champlain; passes by North Hero State Park and the St. Anne Shrine

Vermont 22A, between Vergennes and Fair Haven—in the autumn, is the perfect opportunity to see Vermont's famous fall foliage; passes by many green pastures filled with Vermont dairy cows; also passes nearby Fort Ticonderoga

Skiing the Green Mountains

Skiing is a big deal in Vermont; there are more than 10 alpine ski resorts in the state.

Ascutney Mountain Resort, Brownsville—located on 3,144-foot (958-meter) tall Mount Ascutney

Bromley Mountain, Manchester Center—one of Vermont's oldest ski areas; one of the first ski resorts to roll snow and use snowmaking machinery

Smugglers Notch—located in the area named for the Vermonters who smuggled beef cattle to Canada during the War of 1812; home of a "top-notch" ski school

Mad River Glen, Waitsfield—the only ski mountain in the U.S. actually owned by skiers; skiers who loved the mountain bought it from the retiring owner

Jay Peak, Jay—Vermont's northernmost ski area; home of Vermont's only aerial tramway; favorite of Quebec skiers

Okemo Mountain, Ludlow—during the Great Depression, was one of the areas chosen by the Civilian Conservation Corps to both create jobs for young people and to stimulate use of natural resources

Killington-Pico, Killington—the crown jewel of the American Ski Company; seven lofty snow-covered peaks, with more than 250 trails and 40 ski lifts

Animals

VERMONT'S ANIMALS INCLUDE:

White-tailed Deer
Coyote
Red Fox
Snowshoe Hare
Raccoon
Squirrel
Woodchuck
Porcupine
Bear
Beaver
Otter
Moose
Skunk
Lynx
Pine Marten

Most of the year, snowshoe hares are brown with white marking on their chins, bellies, and tails. In the winter, snowshoe hares shed their brown coats and grow a totally white coat (except for black ear tips)!

Wildlife Watch

Take a Walk on the Wild Side!

Some endangered and threatened animals in Vermont are:

Indiana Bat
Bald Eagle
Canada Lynx
Eastern Puma
Puritan Tiger Beetle
Dwarf Wedgemussel

Some endangered and threatened plants in Vermont are:

Jesup's Milk-vetch
Northeastern Bulrush

Lynxes are wild cats that can weigh up to 45 pounds (20 kilograms)!

Wildlife Watch

Birds

You
may spy
these

birds
in
Vermont:

Raven
Canada Jay
Saw-whet Owl
Oriole
Cardinal
Chickadee
Robin
Finch
Grosbeak
Woodpecker
Nuthatch
Hummingbird
Bluebird
Martin
Quail
Goose
Loon
Thrush

A hummingbird's
wings beat 75
times a second—
so fast that you
only see a blur!
They make short
squeaky sounds,
but do not sing.

Birds

Insects

Don't let these Vermont bugs bug you!

Mayfly
Damselfly
Cricket
Walking Stick
Termite
Giant Water Bug
Spittlebug
Ant Lion
Ground Beetle
Whirligig Beetle
Stag Beetle
Weevil

Monarch Butterfly

Firefly

Ladybug

Grasshopper

Do we know any of these bugs?

Maybe... Hey, that ladybug is cute!

Whirligig beetles have two pairs of eyes—one pair looks above the water, the other under it!

Fish

Perch
Trout
Bream
Eel
Salmon
Catfish
Sheepshead
Carp

Fish

Pond Critters

Hydra
Leech
Freshwater Mussel
Water Flea
Freshwater Crayfish
Fishing Spider
Dragonfly
Giant Water Bug
Back Swimmer
Water Strider
Mosquito
Minnow

Doctors once used leeches to cure illness. They thought the leech would suck out the disease!

Pond
Critters

Rocks and Minerals

Minerals are the building blocks of all rocks. A mineral can be as large as a person, but most are tiny and you will need a magnifying glass to see them clearly. Below are a few types of minerals that can be found in Vermont.

Olivine
Augite
Hornblende
Calcite
Feldspar
Hematite
Quartz
Calcite

Rocks are solid masses of minerals or rock fragments that occur in nature. Below are a few types of rock that can be found in Vermont.

Rocks and Minerals

Most of the world's iron comes from hematite!

Slate
Meteorites
Chert
Flint
Schist

TREEMENDOUS!

THESE TREES TOWER OVER VERMONT!

MAPLE
ASH
CEDAR
BEECH
BIRCH
OAK
ELM
TAMARACK
PINE
SPRUCE
FIR
HEMLOCK

Trees

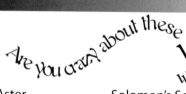

Are you crazy about these **Vermont** wildflowers?

Aster
Lupine
Trillium
Jack-in-the-pulpit
Pitcher Plant
Bog Orchid

Solomon's Seal
Wild Geranium
Columbine
Lady's Slipper
Jacob's Ladder
Wood Anemone

Wildflowers

Red trilliums look pretty, but smell terrible! Their rotten meat odor attracts flies that pollinate the plant.

Flower Power!

Cream of the Crops

Agricultural products from Vermont:

Maple Syrup

Dairy Cattle

Apples

Hay

Sweet Corn

Eggs

Christmas Trees

Milk

Cheese

Poultry

Cream of the Crops

First/Big/Small/Etc.

Vermont became the home of the **first commercially practical ski tow** in 1934.

The **first chairlift** was used on Mount Mansfield in 1940.

Montpelier is the **smallest state capital** in the United States.

The **first postage stamp** used in America was made in Brattleboro in 1846.

East Fairfield is the home of the **first Head Start Program,** used to prepare disadvantaged preschool kids for elementary school.

Dr. H. Nelson Jackson was the **first person to cross the entire United States by automobile;** he started out from Burlington in 1902.

The **first marble quarry** was established at East Dorset in 1785 by Isaac Underhill.

The **first pulp paper mill** was established in Bellows Falls in 1869 by William A. Russell; Russell was also the **first president** of the International Paper Company.

First/Big/Small/Etc.

Celebrate!!!

Stowe Winter Carnival—January

Town Meeting Day, statewide—
first Tuesday in March

Vermont Maple Festival,
St. Albans—April

Vermont Dairy Festival, Enosburg–June

Antique Gas and Steam Engine Show,
Browningtown—June

Old-Time Fiddlers Contest, Hardwick—July

Vermont Quilt Festival, Northfield—July

Arts Festival on the Green, Middlebury—July

Vermont Mozart Festival, Burlington—
July–August

Foliage Festivals,
statewide—
mid-September to mid-October

Holidays

Calendar

Martin Luther King, Jr. Day, *3rd Monday in January*	Groundhog Day *February 2*	Presidents' Day, *3rd Monday in February*
Memorial Day, *last Monday in May*	Independence Day, *July 4*	Labor Day, *1st Monday in September*
Columbus Day *2nd Monday in October*	Veterans Day, *November 11*	Thanksgiving, *4th Thursday in November*

Vermont celebrates its admission to the U.S. on March 4.

Christmas, Chanukah, Kwanzaa, Vietnamese Tet, and Chinese New Year are all holiday celebrations in Vermont.

Famous Food

Vermont is famous for... the following foods!

Sugar on snow
New England boiled dinner
Ben & Jerry's ice cream
Maple syrup
Scotcheroos
Pumpkin pie
Baked squash

Roasted turkey
Shepherd's pie
Baked beans
Sticky buns
Succotash
Chicken in herb sauce
Snickerdoodles

Yum, yum. This is great!

Let's dig in!

Famous Food

Vermont Works!

Vermont has a diverse economy with several major industries including:

Agriculture

About one-fifth of Vermont is farmland, much of which is devoted to dairy farming. Farmers also raise sheep, beef cattle, and other livestock. Of course, maple syrup is a main part of Vermont's economy, as well as vegetables and fruit (especially potatoes and apples).

Mining

Granite is Vermont's biggest mining product, but the state also quarries marble, limestone, sand and gravel, slate, and talc. Much of the marble comes from the western part of the state. Granite is quarried near Barre, Newport, and Randolph.

Tourism has become more important as winter sports have expanded and Vermont roads have improved.

Manufacturing

Vermonters build electrical equipment, fabricated metals, and aircraft engines. Publishing and printing are also important, as well as food processing (especially cheese and other dairy products), and the manufacture of semiconductors.

My First Book About Vermont by Carole Marsh
America the Beautiful: Vermont by Sylvia McNair
Kids Learn America by Patricia Gordon and Reed C. Snow
Let's Discover the States: Vermont by the Aylesworths
The Vermont Experience Series by Carole Marsh

COOL VERMONT WEBSITES

http://www.state.vt.us

http://www.thevermontexperience.com

http://www.50states.com

http://www.netstate.com

Vermont
Glossary

abolitionist: a person opposed to slavery

auditor: a person who examines and checks business accounts

cavalry: soldiers who fight on horseback

constitution: a document outlining the role of a government

emancipation: the act of being set free

igneous: rock formed by the cooling and solidification of magma (melted rock)

metamorphic: rock that has been changed by heat, moisture, and pressure

petroglyphs: ancient rock carvings

potash: made from various minerals and used in making soap, fertilizer, and glass

revolution: the overthrow of a government

secede: to voluntarily give up being a part of an organized group

township: a part of a county having certain powers of local government

Vermont
Spelling Bee

Here are some special Vermont-related words to learn! To take the Spelling Bee, have someone call out the words and you spell them aloud or write them on a piece of paper.

SPELLING WORDS

Abenaki	foliage
abolition	granite
Algonquian	Hubbardton
Ascutney	Iroquois
Bennington	literature
Burlington	manufacturing
cavalry	Montpelier
Champlain	republic
economy	statehood
flatlander	Winooski

Spelling List

ABOUT THE AUTHOR...

CAROLE MARSH has been writing about Vermont for more than 20 years. She is the author of the popular *Vermont State Stuff Series* for young readers and creator along with her son, Michael Marsh, of *Vermont Facts and Factivities,* a CD-ROM widely used in Vermont schools. The author of more than 100 Vermont books and other supplementary educational materials on the state, Marsh is currently working on a new collection of Vermont materials for young people. Marsh correlates her Vermont materials to the Vermont learning standards. Many of her books and other materials have been inspired by or requested by Vermont teachers and librarians.

EDITORIAL ASSISTANT:
Antoinette R. Miller

GRAPHIC DESIGNERS:
Victoria DeJoy   Lisa Stanley   Al Fortunatti